Introduction

This book introduces another unique cu
complements the Lace Flower, first seen
make very delicate leaf-like shapes whic
applications.

GU00720461

There are a few more delightful ideas for
there are eight other beautiful flowers for you to practise your skills on,
presented in Pat Ashby's inimitably easy step by step format.

An opportunity has arisen to show the work of some of the British
Sugarcraft Guild Cygnets (under 16's), whose ingenuity and patience is
notable.

Pat was so impressed with Alice Overington's Cosmos and Gypsophila
that we **had** to show them to you.

Templates of the other cutters referred to in the book are shown on Pages
37 to 39.

The Tools. General Notes: Non-stick. One of their most useful aspects is
their non-stick property, which is inherent in the design and material used.
It is not a surface finish and, therefore, cannot wear off. It also means they
cut cleanly, without fuzzy edges.

Materials. All the tools can be used with any soft material such as
flowerpaste, sugarpaste, Permapaste, marzipan, modelling chocolate,
plasticine, modelling clay, etc.

Temperature. Normally hand washing in warm soapy water is all that is
required. They will withstand boiling water or the dishwasher without
deforming.

Handles. All the cutters have handles or fit comfortably into your hand,
which allows you to exert firm pressure over the whole of the cutting
edges. Stability. They will not rust, corrode, deform or wear out with normal
usage. They should NOT be 'scrubbed' on the board or twisted.

Marking. All the tools are permanently marked to aid easy identification.

Metal. The cutters are delicate and should not be brought into contact with
sharp metal objects which may damage the cutting edges or surfaces. i.e.
keep them separated from metal cutters.

Hygiene. The materials meet the appropriate EEC regulations for food
hygiene.

Endorsement. All the items are personally endorsed and used by PAT
ASHBY, our Technical Director, who is one of the leading teachers of
sugarcraft in the UK and is an international judge, author and demonstrator.

The New Lace Leaf Cutters (LL1, LL2, LL3, LL4)

(Full size cut-out shapes are shown in Illustration 3).
These designs follow on from the Lace Flowers and use the same idea but as an outlined leaf shape. The overall shape is not symmetrical so that they make an alternative leaf when turned over. Their delicate appearance adds a touch of elegance to any spray or top decoration.

How to make the Lace Leaves *(See Illustration 4)*

1. Roll out White or coloured flowerpaste* thinly and press down firmly with any of the 4 Lace Leaf Cutters (LL1, LL2, LL3, LL4) – run your fingers over the outer points of the cutter – then lift straight up. 'Scrubbing' or twisting the cutter is not required and may damage it. Remove the surplus material including the centre hole cutouts, twist the leaf to the shape required and leave to dry.

2. If the leaf is to be wired, roll out the paste over the shallow end of a groove on an Orchard green grooved board and position the base of the cutter over the groove before cutting out. (See Illustration 5).

Moisten the end of a 26 or 33 gauge wire and push gently into the thickened portion of the leaf. Leave to dry.

3. When dry, dust with an appropriate Orchard petal dust and 'steam' by passing the leaf briefly through the steam from a boiling kettle or similar. Alternatively,dip or paint with an edible varnish.

*These cutters, as with all Orchard cutters, can be used very effectively with an airdrying non-edible paste such as Orchard 'Permapaste'.

66 mm   LL1

54 mm   LL2

47 mm   LL3

40 mm   LL4

6

7

How to make the Cake Top Decoration *(See Illustration 6)*

1. Roll out White pastillage and cut out 20 Lace Leaves LL3. Remove the centre cutouts. Lay out the leaves alternating in gently curving lines of 5 leaves each on a flat surface (preferably wood to assist drying out) and overlap the points of the leaves, glueing in position with paste glue. (See Illustration 7 and Template 7A). Trim the base of the columns to leave a flatish surface when assembled.
When dry, tip the leaves with a petal dust of choice – in this case Rubine.

2. Cot. Cut out 8 more White LL4 leaves and place 4 in an apple tray, overlapping and glueing their bases.
Put a blob of paste glue in the centre and place the remaining 4 leaves in the centre spread out a little, propping them with cloud drift. Leave to dry.
When dry, tip the leaves with petal dust – colour of choice.

3. Stand. Set 3 White LL1 leaves into an apple tray, overlap and glue their bases together. When dry turn them over to form a three legged stand for the cot. Place a tiny baby in the cot. This assembly to be placed under the centre of the decoration.

4. Optionally, cover a 6 inch dia. board with sugarpaste – pastel colouring of choice. Leave to dry.

5. Assembly. Glue two of the columns together at the top while flat on the board. When dry, stand them up on the cake board or cake, glueing the bases to the board with paste glue, and prop with film containers or similar. Apply paste glue to the top and bottom of a third column and stand up on the board, positioned at right angles to the first two. Prop with film containers.
Repeat the above for the fourth column, opposite the third, and leave to dry.

6. Flower. Make a lace leaf flower and glue on the top. Cut out 8 more White LL3 leaves and place 4 in an apple tray, overlapping and glueing their bases.
Put a blob of paste glue in the centre and place the remaining 4 leaves in the centre more or less upright, propping them with cloud drift. Glue a few Yellow stamens into the centre. Leave to dry.
When dry, tip the leaves with petal dust – colour of choice.
A second baby can be placed in the flower, if required.

Template 7A

8

9

How to make the Fairy Christmas Tree *(See Illustration 8)*

1. Make a Red tub about ³/₄" dia. and ¹/₂" high from flowerpaste/sugarpaste or Almond paste. Mark a circle round the side with a knife. Push a 4" length approx. of 24 gauge wire (or the finest variety of spaghetti) into the top to make a hole. Remove the wire and leave the tub to dry thoroughly. Place a small ball of Green flowerpaste onto a firm base, such as a 4" square of polystyrene, and push the wire through the paste and into the firm base to hold it steady while assembling.

2. Roll out Green flowerpaste and cut out 1 – Lace flower (LF1). Remove the centre of the sepals. 'Glue' (rose water, Gum Arabic or egg white) the ball of paste and thread the centre of the LF1 down the wire. Prop under the centre of the sepals with a little 'cloud drift'* to create a gentle curve. Slide a small ball of Green paste down the wire. (See Illustration 9).

3. Repeat Step 2 twice, interleaving the sepals.

4. Cut out 3 – Lace flowers (LF2) and repeat, separating them with small balls of Green paste on the wire, and with 'cloud drift'.

5. Cut out 2 – Lace flowers each (LF3 and LF4) and proceed similarly.

6. Cut out 1 – LF4, turn the paste over and slide onto the wire. Bend the points of the sepals upwards and join together on the wire with glue. Trim the wire, leaving enough to attach the star.

7. Cut out a White calyx R13A and attach to the top of the wire with glue.

Leave to dry thoroughly.

8. Transfer the tree to the tub by holding the star.

9. Cover a 4" dia. board with Red sugarpaste and mark by rolling a hair curler or ribbed roller over it to represent a carpet. Glue the tub and tree onto the board.

9. If desired, when dry, decorate the tree with piped loops and bulbs of White Royal Icing (0 tube) and paint with the Orchard range of edible colours as required.

* *'Cloud drift' is artificial fibre as found in duvets, or stuffed toys.*

11

10

How to make the Decorative Baubles *(See Illustration 10)*

(from an idea by Moira Downie, Zimbabwe)

1. Cut out 2 – Lace Flowers (LF1, LF2 or LF3) from White or coloured flowerpaste and place them in or on circular formers about 2 to 2½" dia. (Plastic Christmas tree baubles that split in half are ideal). Leave to nearly dry out. (See Illustration 11).

2. Hook the end of a 26 gauge wire by making a small loop and bending over at right angles. Make a small hole in the centre of an apple tray or use a similar sized plastic former.

3. Attach a small ball of paste glue to the inside centre of one of the Lace Flowers, and thread the wire through the centre with the hook inside. Attach the wire and thread through the hole in the apple tray.

4. Attach the points of the second Lace Flower to the points of the first Lace Flower with paste glue. Overlap a little for strength. Adjust to a circular shape. Leave to dry completely.

5. If required, paint with Orchard Majestic Gold or Rubine or Pool Blue.

6. Small items, such as a sugarpaste candle, can be attached with paste glue inside.

12

13

14

How to make the Lace Flower Spray *(See Illustration 12)*

1. Centre. Tape about 9 long stamens onto a 26 gauge wire.

Roll out Green flowerpaste and cut out 2 Calyxes (R11C). Place on the Orchard Pad and vein each sepal from the tip to the centre (See Illustration 13). Glue the centre of the first one and place the second on top, interleaving the sepals. (See Illustration 14).

2. Flower. (See Illustration 16). Roll out Red flowerpaste and cut out 2 Lace flowers (LF4). Remove the centre petals* with the pointed end of the Petal Veining Tool (OP2) starting at the wider end of each petal so as not to damage the tips and place on the pad. (See Illustration 15). Ball the edges of the petals and cup by balling from the tip to the base.

'Glue' the centre of the first flower and place the second flower on top interleaving the sepals. Glue the centre of the calyxes from Step 1, place the flowers on top while flat, interleaving the sepals, and transfer the whole assembly to the flowerstand. Prop with 'cloud drift' to achieve a suitable cup shape.

3. Mash down some of the Red paste (it should be like chewing gum) and place some in the middle of the flower. Place the base of the first petal* in between the sepals of the flower and continue for the first row of 5. Repeat with a second row of petals **inside** the first row, alternating as you go. (See Illustration 16).

4. 'Glue' the base of the stamens and thread the wire through the centre of the flower. Leave to dry.

Leaves. (See Illustration 17).

5. Hook the end of a 33 gauge wire.

Roll out Green flowerpaste and cut out one Lace Flower (LF4). Cut across the base of each section to form a leaf shape. 'Glue' the top of the wire and press into the underside of the base of the leaf. Squeeze. Leave in a curved position to dry. When dry dust with Gold Green.

Trio Flowers *(See Illustration 18)*

6. Tape 5 long pointed stamens onto a 26 gauge white wire. (Paint the stamens the same Red as your main flower). Leave to dry.

7. Roll out White flowerpaste and position the Lace flower cutter (LF4) near the edge to cut out only 3 sections. Remove the centre petals. 'Glue' the base of the stamens and press firmly into the centre of the cutout. Wrap petals around the wire, and squeeze at the base. Fan out to a propeller shape.

8. Place into a flower stand to set. Prop with 'cloud drift'. When dry dust the centre with Lime Green and the petals Orchard Satin Silk or similar.

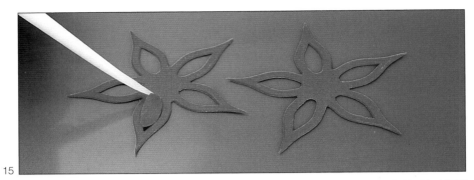

15

16

17

18

19

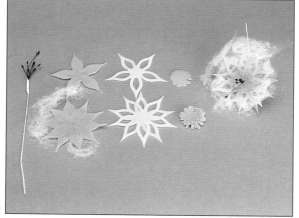

20

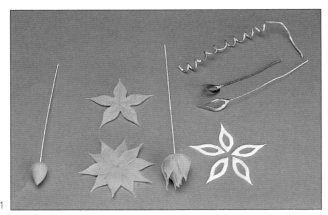

How to make the Hanging Spray *(See Illustration 19)*

This is a spray made up with a different version of the Lace Flower.

1. Centre. Tape 8 short and 1 long Brown (or colour of choice) stamens to the end of a 26 gauge wire.

2. Flower. Cut out 2 Orange calyxes (R11C) as for Step 1 Page 11.
Cut out 2 Yellow petals (LF4), remove the centre petals and dispose.
'Glue' the centre of the calyxes and interleave the first petal (LF4) on top.
Repeat with the second petal. Prop with 'cloud drift'. (See Illustration 20).
Cut out 2 Orange carnations C2, frill with the plain frilling tool FT1 and glue into the centre of the flower. Glue the base of the stamens in Step 1 and thread the centre wire through the centre of the flower. Leave to dry.

3. Half-open Bud. Repeat Step 2 and press Yellow tips together.

4. Buds. (See Illustration 21). Press a cone of Orange flowerpaste onto the end of a 'glued' 28 gauge wire and leave to dry. Cut out 2 Orange calyxes R11C, glue them together interleaved, glue the cone and thread them up the wire. Wrap round the cone, leaving the tips standing out a little.

5. Leaves. Make 5 White leaves as in Step 5 Page 11. When dry, paint them with Majestic Gold dust or colour of choice.

6. The Frond. Wind a piece of White 28 gauge wire round a knitting needle or similar, slide off and then paint with Majestic Gold or colour of choice.

7. Butterfly. Make as in Book 8, summarized here. Roll out White flowerpaste, cut across the centre, lift one piece and overlap it slightly with the other. Cut out 1 butterfly B2 over the join and dust with Orchard Blue petal dust. Steam. When dry, scratch some veins through the blue colour with a pin or sharp scalpel.
Pipe a body with Brown Royal Icing into the V of a piece of folded card and press the wings into the body. Leave to dry.

8. Assembly. Tape about 3 flowers, 4 buds, 20 leaves and 3 fronds into a spray and suspend from a Black wire 'C' shaped frame.

22

How to make the Nerium Oleander *(See Illustration 22)*

Oleander are grown for their profuse showy flowers in every shade of pink, plus apricot, crimson and white. Some varieties are fragrant.

Native to the Mediterranean, Africa, Asia & Japan.

1. Centre cone.

Pop a small ball of Cream flowerpaste onto the end of a White 24 gauge wire and roll between finger and thumb to make a long cone – about the length of the calyx sepal. Mark narrow diagonal lines around the cone to represent a twisted cylinder.

2. Make a Mexican Hat of White flowerpaste with the Mexican Hat Adaptor (M1). Roll out the brim to thin the paste and cut out one calyx R13. Roll out the sepals sideways slightly to widen. Place on the Orchard Pad (PD1) and soften each sepal with the balling tool (OP1). Cut each sepal lengthways into very fine strips with scissors. Hollow out the centre with the petal veining tool (OP2). Form into a cup shape. Separate the sections before painting with the pointed end of the veining tool (OP2).

While the paste is still soft, dust the base of the centre with Orchard Yellow Glo, and paint Carmine streaks from the base out to the tips with a 00 paintbrush. (See Illustration 23).

3. Glue the base of the centre cone from Step 1 and thread the wire through the middle of the throat of the centre calyx. Pop into the flowerstand and feather the sections by separating with the pointed end of the veining tool (OP2). Leave to dry. Tape on another 24 gauge wire for strength.

4. Flower. Make a Mexican Hat, using the largest hole of M1, with White flowerpaste and roll out the brim to thin the paste. Cut out one Five-petal flower F6. Elongate each petal with the Slimpin (flap up the petals on either side temporarily). Move to the Pad (PD1) and vein each petal with the petal veining tool (OP2). Soften the edges by pressing hard with the balling tool (OP1).

5. Hollow out the centre of the flower with the veining tool (OP2), glue the base of the dried centre from Step 3 and thread through the centre of the flower. Press around the base to form the trumpet and roll between your fingers to elongate the trumpet. Leave to dry. (See Illustration 24).

6. Calyx. Roll out Lime Green flowerpaste and cut out one R15 calyx. Dust the base and tips Carmine. Glue the base of the flower, thread the calyx onto the wire and press gently round the base.

7. Bud. Pop a small ball of Cream flowerpaste onto the end of a 26 gauge wire and roll between finger and thumb to make a long cone. Mark 4 narrow grooves around the cone. The buds are of different sizes.

Turn upside down and snip tiny triangles at the base of the cone with scissors to represent the calyx.

Dust the base with Lime Green and the top with Rubine. Paint the grooves with Carmine. (See Illustration 25).

8. Tiny Bud. Glue the end of a 26 gauge wire and attach a tiny ball of White flowerpaste.

Roll out Lime Green flowerpaste and cut out one R15 calyx. Thread the wire through the centre of the calyx and wrap round the ball of paste.

Paint the base with Carmine.

9. Leaves. Attach a ball of Lime Green flowerpaste to a 26 gauge wire and roll between your hands to elongate it down the wire. Press out from either side of the wire with your fingers to flatten it. Roll with the Slimpin to make it finer. Cut to shape following Illustration 25.

Roll the veining tool (OP2) to vein the leaf and mark a centre vein with the pointed end.

How to make the Plumbago flower *(See Illustration 26)*

Use as a medium sized filler flower with an Orchid baby's breath etc.

1. Stem. Insert a small ball of White flowerpaste about ¼" down a 33 gauge White wire. Do not glue the wire as the covering tends to unravel.

Roll between finger and thumb to start, then transfer to the palm of your hand and continue rolling with three fingers spread out, to make a long back, at least an 1" long. The paste should be just hanging over the end of the wire. Make a tiny platform at the top by indenting with the small end of the balling tool (OP1). (See Illustration 27).

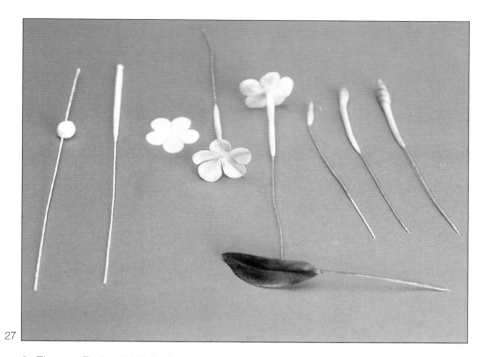

2. Flower. Roll out White flowerpaste and cut out one Five-petal flower F10.
Vein each petal with the veining tool OP2. Mark a centre vein down each petal. Soften the edges with the balling tool (OP1). Turn over.

Glue the top of the platform from Step 1 and place in the centre of the flower. Make a tiny hole in the centre, put a little glue in the centre and insert 5 tiny stalks of Blue stamens. Dust the base of the long back Pale Green and the remainder Pale Blue. Dust the flower Pale Blue with a tinge of Alpine Rose.

Paint the centre veins Dark Blue.

3. Bud. Push a 33 gauge White wire through a small ball of White flowerpaste, making a cone at the top and then thinning it down the wire, rolling it in the palm of your hand.

Place the cone on your forefinger and mark the cone with a knife, giving a spiral effect for the bigger buds. Gently curve the wire.

The long buds are the same length as the back of the flower.

The smaller buds are half the length of the back of the flower.

Dust $^3/_4$" of the length of the tapered sausage Lime Green and the top Light Blue. Gently curve the top of the wire.

4. Tiny buds are about $^1/_4$" long, and are Green with Red/Brown tips. Gently curve the wire.

28

How to make the Pride of India Flower (Crepe Myrtle) *(See Illustration 28)*
from an idea by Jillean Crouch of Australia.

This is a shrub native to India. The flowers come in shades of white, lavender, mauve, pink, purple, and crimson and appear in the summer in countries like Australia, China, India, South Africa, Zimbabwe etc.

1. Six petals required. Roll out flowerpaste – colour of choice – and insert a fine White wire into the edge of the paste. Continue to thin out taking care not to allow the wire to show. Cut out a petal with a carnation cutter C2 over the wire position.

Frill the edge all round and bend side edges of petal upwards and curve top of petal downward. Leave to dry.

2. Centre. You will need about 40 stamen heads. Wrap two pieces of wire round the centre of the stamens so you can cut through the middle to get two centres for the flower. Cut off one end of one stamen so that it is full length and push in right through the centre. (See Illustration 29).

Cut off both ends of six stamens and curve over your finger. Tape round the centre evenly spaced. This is attached to a 26 gauge wire. Trim ends of stamens at the base and tape securely to the wire.

29

30

3. Fix petals regularly round the centre with florists tape with lower edge of petals on a level with the top of the Yellow stamens and tape to the bottom of their wires.

4. Calyx. Make a Mexican hat with Lime Green flowerpaste in the second smallest hole of the Mexican Hat adaptor (M1), roll out the brim and cut out a calyx with the Six-petal cutter N7. Put a little fat on the end of the veining tool (OP2) and press into the centre of the calyx and widen each sepal.

Moisten the base of the centre and thread the calyx onto the wire.

5. Position petals of the calyx in V's and curve stamens in line with points of calyx. Bend petals at right angles to their wires. Twist so that the centre vein of petals run horizontally round the flower on a level with the top of the stamens.

6. Buds. Thread a small ball of White flowerpaste onto a hooked 26 gauge Green wire. Press into the top with the tiny Six-petal cutter N8 to make indentations. Squeeze down each side with tweezers to make six grooves. Dust the top with the appropriate colour – Mauve, etc. – and the base with Pale Moss Green. 'Steam' to set the colours. (See Illustration 30).

7. Leaves. The leaves are oval and different sizes and wired with 33 gauge wire. Colour – Lime Green and dust with a darker Green.

31

32

Template 32A

How to make the Wax Geraldton Flower (Chamalaucium uncinatum) *(See Illustration 31)*

The shrub is a native of Western Australia. In the UK it is used as a filler flower in bouquets.

1. Press a small ball of White flowerpaste into the second smallest hole in the Mexican Hat Adaptor (M1). Roll out the brim and cut out an F2L blossom. Cut out a wedge shape at the base of each petal – See Template 32A. Move to the Orchard Pad (PD1) and soften the edges of the petals.

2. Glue the hooked end of a 33 gauge Green wire and thread through the centre of the petal. Make a hole in the centre with the Petal Veining Tool (OP2). The back of the Mexican Hat can be left quite wide and mark one or two grooves in it. Paint these Lime Green and the base of the flower Burgundy. Dust the inside of the flower Lime Green. Add 3 Pale Burgundy spots around the base of the petals in a triangular formation. (See Illustration 32).

3. The flowers can be taped together in groups of 4 with, sometimes, an odd flower.

4. Buds. Pop a small ball of White flowerpaste onto a Green 33 gauge wire, roll between finger and thumb to make a squashed cone shape. Colour the rounded top (fattest end) Dark Burgundy (with a touch of Black). The base of the bud tapers and is coloured Pale Lime Green. Lime Green stalk.

As the buds get bigger they are pale pink (Dusty Rose) with a Lime Green base. Some of the small Burgundy buds have Burgundy stems.

5. Leaves. The leaves are described as narrow and needlelike.

Take ¼ width Green florists tape in one hand and roll the end between finger and thumb to form a wirelike shape. Cut into short lengths (1"), flatten and trim top to a point. (See Illustration 33).

Tape onto a Green 26 gauge wire alternately.

33

How to make the Yesterday, Today and Tomorrow Flower
(Brunfelsia Pauciflora) *(See Illustration 34)*

This flower is a native of Brazil. It is grown for the exquisitely scented flowers which cover the bush from late winter to early spring.

The flowers are violet-mauve when they open and fade to pale mauve and then white on successive days.

1. Stem. Insert a small ball of White flowerpaste about ¼" down a 24 gauge White wire. Do not glue the wire as the covering tends to unravel.

Roll between finger and thumb to start, then transfer to the palm of your hand and continue rolling with three fingers spread out, to make a long back, at least an 1" long. The paste should be just hanging over the end of the wire. Make a tiny platform at the top by indenting with the small end of the balling tool (OP1). (See Illustration 35).

2. Roll out White flowerpaste and cut out one F5 Five-petal flower. Place on the Orchard Pad (PD1) and lightly vein the petals with the veining tool (OP2). Soften the edges with the balling tool. Turn over and ball inside the outside edge. Glue the top of the platform from Step 1 and press into the centre of the flower. Turn the flower over and form a hole in the centre with the fluted end of the veining tool (OP2).

3. There is a White patch around the centre and the remainder can be dusted with Mauve, Pale Mauve or left White. (There is a tiny White pistil and five Mauve stamens with Yellow tips which can be glued to a small hole in the centre of the flower, but these are not normally visible since they do not extend above the centre hole and, therefore, I have omitted them).

4. Calyx. Roll out Lime Green flowerpaste with a touch of Brown. Cut out one R15 calyx. Cut off the tips, glue the base of the flower and thread onto the wire. Press the sepals close together.

5. Bud. Push a small fat oval ball of White flowerpaste onto the end of a 26 gauge Green wire and pinch five grooves with tweezers. Paint the grooves Brown. Small buds are Lime Green. (See Illustration 36).

6. Seed pod. Attach a small Brown ball of flowerpaste to the end of a 24 gauge wire. Leave to dry. Roll out Green flowerpaste and cut out an R15 calyx for the small pods and an R13A for the larger ones. Glue the base of the pod and thread the calyx up the wire and wrap round the pod.

7. Leaves. The leaves are long ovals in all sizes ranging from Pale Lime Green to Dark Green.

36

37

How to make the Pandorea Jasminoides 'Rosea' *(See Illustration 37)*

This evergreen vine is native to Australia, Malaysia and Zimbabwe. It comes in white with a carmine throat and pink.

1. Centre Pistil. Cut ⅓ width of White florists tape and wrap round the end of a 26 gauge wire - keeping the tape in the same position. Dust with Lemon Glo petal dust.

2. Flower. Make a Mexican Hat with White flowerpaste using the largest hole in the Mexican Hat Adaptor (M1) and roll out the brim. Cut out a petal with the Five-petal cutter F5. Pop onto the Orchard 'Paddy' Pad (PDH) using again the largest hole, and vein each petal with the veining tool (OP2). Soften the edges of the petals with the balling tool (OP1) – flap up the petals either side temporarily to make that job a little easier.

Grease the stem of the flower with Trex (so that it does not dry out too quickly). Likewise dip the fluted end of the veining tool into fat (Trex) and hollow out the throat of the flower, pressing it firmly against your finger to thin it out.

3. 'Glue' the base of the pistil and thread through the centre of the flower. Put fat on your fingers and gently taper the paste down the wire, twisting and pressing. (See Illustration 38).

4. Calyx. Should the flower be wanted for a bouquet, turn the flower upsidedown and snip five V's to represent a calyx. Leave to dry in the flowerstand (S1), propped with cloud drift.

Alternatively, cut out one Green calyx R15, glue the base of the flower, thread the calyx up the wire and attach.

5. When dry, dust the centre base of the flower Lemon Glo, then deep Alpine Rose. The petals are pale Alpine Rose. The back of the flower has a deep Alpine Rose streak on the lefthand side of each petal

6. Buds. Push a fat cone of White flowerpaste onto the end of a 26 gauge wire and taper both ends. Make lengthways indentations around the cone with a knife to represent petals about to unfurl.

The calyx is the same as Step 4.

7. Leaves. These are Dark Green oval, heavily veined, of different sizes on 26 gauge wire. Dust and steam, since they have a glossy finish.

8. The top of the cake in Illustration 37 is also decorated with White Lace Leaves, dusted Green and Alpine Rose.

38

39

How to make the Cosmos *(See Illustration 39)*

by Alice Overington

1. Centre. Loop the end of a 28 gauge wire round the centre of 15 stamens and fold them in half. Use $\frac{1}{2}$ width florists tape to secure. Paint the base of the stamens with the colour of choice and tip some of the stamens.

2. Roll out White flowerpaste onto the grooved board, slightly thicker than normal, and cut out eight rose petals R2. To make them slightly narrower, move the cutter a little to the left and cut again; then to the right and cut again. (See Illustration 40). Elongate the petal slightly with the balling tool Push a 28 gauge wire a little way into the stem, twisting as you go to prevent unravelling of the covering.

Vein with the veining tool (OP2) or a cosmos veiner, soften the edges and draw out 3 flutes with a small balling tool or dresden tool. (See Illustration 41). Leave to dry. Dust with an Orchard petal dust – colour of choice.

3. Tape two petals opposite each other onto the centre stamens. Keeping the tape in the same position, add two more petals at right angles to the first pair. Then add the remaining four petals in between the first four. Tape down the wire, adding another 28 gauge wire for strength.

4. Calyx. Roll out Green flowerpaste and cut out one daisy DY5. Soften the sepals with the balling tool. Glue the base of the flower and slide the calyx up the wire, pressing it under the petals.

Roll out 8 equal thin Green spikes of flowerpaste about $\frac{1}{2}$" long. One way of ensuring you have an equal amount of paste for each one is to cut out a Fuchsia calyx FS2 and cut each sepal in half lengthways. These are then stuck vertically under the calyx positioned in between the sepals.

5. Twist florists Green tape into needle shaped leaves and tape onto the stem in random fashion. (See Illustration 42).

6. Bud. The bud looks like 8 petals folded up with a calyx. Tape two 24 gauge wires together, leaving the ends clear, burn the ends in a lighter flame and push and twist into a ball of White flowerpaste. This seals the paste onto the wire. Emboss the top with a small daisy cutter DY6 and extend each groove by pinching down with tweezers. Glue the base and attach a DY6 Green daisy as a calyx. Position 8 spikes as in Step 4.

Colour the marks with the chosen Orchard petal dust painted on.

These flowers were on display at Squires Kitchen Exhibition in 1997.

40

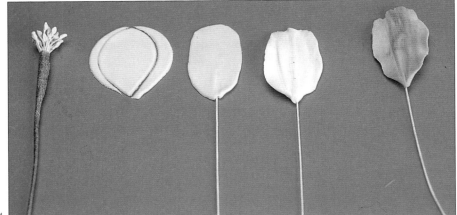

41

42

How to make the Gypsophila *(See Illustration 39)*
by Alice Overington

1. Flower. Roll out White flowerpaste and cut out 5 blossoms F2L. Frill each sepal with a blunted cocktail stick Hook the end of a 30 gauge wire and push the wire through the centre of the flower.

Fold the flower in half – bottom to top, glue in between and fold $\frac{1}{3}$ to top. Turn over and fold $\frac{1}{3}$ to the top. (See Illustration 43).

This will give you a small flower. When dry, paint a tiny 5 sepal Green calyx at the base.

To make a larger flower, proceed as above and leave to dry a little.

Then frill a second petal, glue and cup it underneath the first petal.

2. Calyx. Roll out Green flowerpaste and cut out a R15 calyx. Cut off $2\frac{1}{2}$ sepals and split the remaining 2 to make 5 small sepals. Glue the base of the flower and wrap this calyx around the flower.

OR cut out a six-petal flower N8 and cut off one sepal.

Glue the base of the flower, thread this calyx up the wire and press underneath.

3. Buds. Press a small ball of White paste onto the end of a 33 gauge Green wire – 3 sizes.

Green stamens make the tiny buds.

4. To wire up a spray, try to copy a natural spray of gypsophila.

43

44

How to make the Owl *(See Illustration 44)*

1. Roll out equal quantities of Brown and Cream flowerpaste 'A' (or 50/50 Sugarpaste and flowerpaste) and place one on top of the other.

2. Set the 'Varicut' Cutter to A/C6/D1 and cut out some shapes.

Trim the base across. See Diagram 45.

3. Make two diagonal cuts in the sides for the wings as Diagram 45. and shape the wings as required. Indent the feathers on the wings and body with the cut down end of a drinking straw.

4. Fold over the top to create the beak.

5. The eyes are 2 Brown circles cut with the base of a piping tube, with 2 smaller White circles in the centre and Black pupils piped off-centre.

5. Fold in the two side panels.

6. Attach two small balls of Orange paste to the base as feet. Mark feet with three indentations for claws.

7. To finish, place a small hat on the head made from a flower or a triangle of paste. The figure can be stood on a thin plaque or board covered in sugarpaste and marked with a hair roller to give a carpet effect.

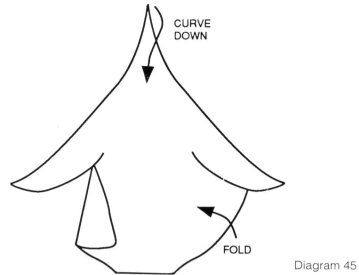

CURVE
DOWN

FOLD

Diagram 45

46

How to make the Oak Leaf Owl *(See Illustration 46)*

This imaginative idea was created by a Cygnet – Hannah Wilson (aged 11) from the Runnymede Branch of the British Sugarcraft Guild.

1. Sketch out the general outline shape of the owl onto an 8" board, covered with sugarpaste.

2. Roll out coloured sugarpaste or flowerpaste thinly and cut out approximately 60 oak leaves of different sizes OL1, OL2 and OL3. Vein with the oak leaf veiners OL5, OL6 & OL7 by pressing each leaf gently onto the appropriate veiner with a soft sponge.

3. While still soft, dust them with Orchard petal dusts of your choice, probably Brown, Green and Red with a little Yellow here and there, using a soft brush.

4. Then place them on the board, starting at the base with the largest ones, within the outline you have already marked.

You can stick them down to the board or to each other with a *little* rose water painted on with a paint brush.

5. When you have put on all the leaves, you can make the eyes from two small balls of Brown sugarpaste, flattened, with a tiny, tiny ball of Black paste in the centre. Paint in some eyelashes with a fine (00) paint brush.

6. The beak is made from a cone of Brown sugarpaste, flattened, cut halfway down and opened out.

How to make the Clown *(See Illustration 47)*

This delightful chap was one of several made by the Cygnets (under 16) of the Norton Radstock Branch of the British Sugarcraft Guild for the Trowbridge Exhibition in 1997. He is made using carnation cutters, sticking the petals together. There are no wires in the model. It is a good idea to work on the arms or legs together so that you can keep the colours the same.

1. Body and Ruff. Roll out White and Rubine and Grey coloured flowerpaste and cut out approx. 10 large carnations C1. Frill them with the frilling tools (FT1-4) and leave to dry. (You can also cut out 40 small carnations C2 in the same way for the arms and legs*).

Cut out 10 more large carnations C1 – 2 or 3 at a time – frill them, and then start assembling the body by placing the C1 flowers on top of each other, alternating between the dry ones and the soft ones. Use a little piped Royal Icing between each one to stick them together. Colours of choice. Leave to dry. For ease of working, stand the body upright and stick it towards the back of a 5" board covered with Grey sugarpaste. The buttons are small balls of sugarpaste indented with a cocktail stick.

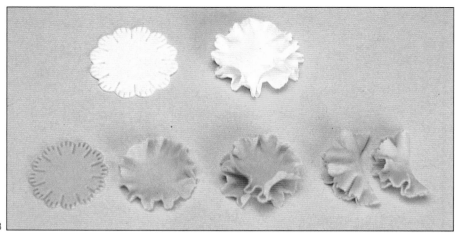

48

2. The Head. Roll out a ball of Skintone coloured flowerpaste about 1" diameter. Leave to dry. The eyes are piped with White Royal Icing and finished with tiny balls of Black flowerpaste. The nose is a small ball of Red flowerpaste stuck on with rose water. Paint the mouth on with a No.1 brush using Orchard Red petal dust mixed with water. Make the hat from a 3" square of rolled out Blue flowerpaste cut diagonally. Fold round into a cone and when dry, attach to the head with Royal Icing. Stick the head to the top of the dried body with Royal Icing. The hair can now be piped on with Orange Royal Icing. Similarly the Yellow and White hat decorations.

3. The Legs. Make 2 boots from Black flowerpaste and pull out the ankle to leave a rounded end. Leave to dry. Cut out 4 White C2 carnations, frill and stick together with Royal Icing. Gently push the ankle of the boot into the frills and leave to dry with the feet in the air. Each leg is made from approx. 16 more C2 carnations, alternating dry and soft petals, stuck together with Royal Icing. The knee joint is formed from three petals folded over in half. (See Illustration 48).

Leave the legs to dry and then attach to the body with Royal Icing and a freshly made carnation so that the join does not show.

4. The Arms. These are made in exactly the same way as the legs, with the hands being pushed into the 4 White petals and allowed to dry. The hands are a cone of Black flowerpaste, flattened, with a V cut out to represent a thumb. Don't forget to get the thumbs the right way round – left and right. The cuffs fold over the hands. The 3 folded petals acting as the elbow. When dry, attach to the body with Royal Icing as before. You may need to prop up the arms with sponge while they dry.

5. The Ball. The rainbow ball is made up of pieces of all the pastes used (except Black) and rolled into a $^3/_4$" dia. ball stuck down with Royal Icing.

* The exact number of petals depends on how much you frill them and how long you want the limbs to be.

LF1
104mm

LF4
70mm

LF2
94mm

LF3
80mm

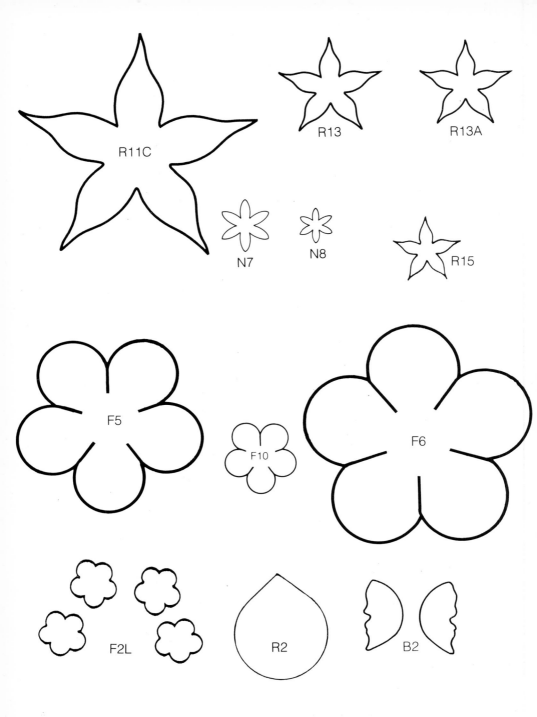

R11C

R13

R13A

N7

N8

R15

F5

F10

F6

F2L

R2

B2

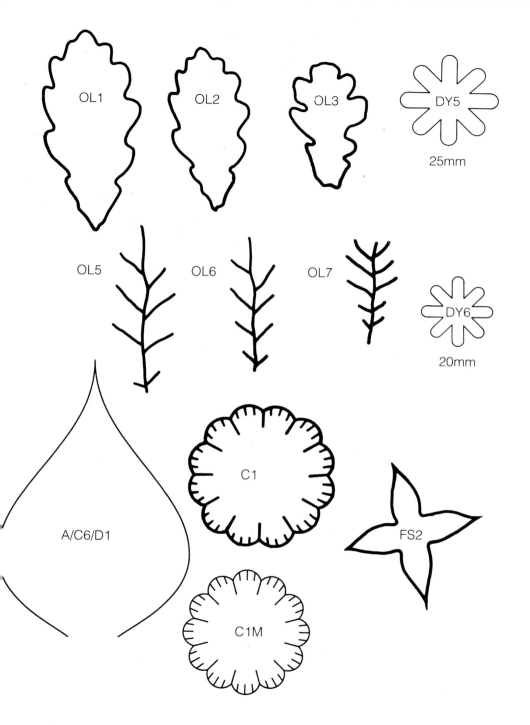

OL1

OL2

OL3

DY5

25mm

OL5

OL6

OL7

DY6

20mm

A/C6/D1

C1

FS2

C1M

RECIPES

Flowerpaste A (or Lace Paste)

250g (½lb) Bakel's Pettinice or Craigmillar's Pastello only.

1 teaspoon (5ml) Gum Tragacanth

Rub 'Trex' on your hands and knead ingredients together until elastic. Wrap tightly in plastic cling film and store in an airtight container. Leave for 24 hours. Store in a cool place. This paste keeps well if worked through, say, once a week. Always keep tightly wrapped.

Flowerpaste D. 450g (1lb) sieved icing sugar

5mls Gum Tragacanth and 20mls CMC (Carboxymethylcellulose) – Tylose

10ml white fat (Trex or Spry, not lard)

10ml powdered Gelatine soaked in 25ml of cold water.

10ml Liquid Glucose

45ml egg white   5ml = 1 teaspoon

Sieve all the icing sugar into a **greased*** (Trex) mixing bowl.Add the gums to the sugar. Warm the mixture in the microwave oven 3 x 50 secs on a medium setting, stirring in between.

Sprinkle the gelatine over the water in a cup and allow to 'sponge'.

Put the cup in hot, not boiling water, until clear. Add the white fat and glucose. Heat the dough hook beater, add the dissolved ingredients and the egg white to the warmed sugar, and beat on the lowest speed until all the ingredients are combined. At this stage the mixture will be a dingy beige colour. Turn the machine to maximum speed and mix until the mixture becomes white and stringy. Grease your hands and remove the paste from the machine. Pull and stretch the paste several times. Knead together and cut into 4 sections. Knead each section again, wrap in clingfilm, and put into a plastic bag, then in an airtight container and keep in the refrigerator. Let it mature for 24 hours. This paste dries quickly so, when ready to use, cut off only a small piece and re-seal the remainder. Work it well with your fingers. It should 'click' between your fingers when ready to use. If it should be a little too hard and crumbly, add a little egg white and fat. The fat slows down the drying process and the egg white makes it more pliable.

Keep coloured paste in a separate container. This paste keeps for several months.

* This eases the strain on the machine considerably.

Pastillage C

Make up 8oz. Royal Icing. Add two teaspoons 'Tylose'. Mix thoroughly. Wrap in cling film and put into an airtight container. Leave 24 hours before working.

Paste Glue. 1oz sugarpaste of the same colour as the items to be glued.

2 dessertspoons of warm water

Gradually combine together and place in the microwave oven for 1-1½ mins until the mixture boils. When cool use as required. Store at room temperature, or refrigerate if not to be used for a length of time.

If the glue is to be used immediately then it is not necessary to boil it.